What a wonderful gift of bringing all areas of a woman's life, feelings, and faith together to walk a path none of us desire to walk. In order to eliminate the disease of cancer in our bodies, strength and stamina are there for us to tap into in the name of the Most High God. Jane has given this gift from *her* life-changing days in the battle in which we are victorious simply because *we are his!*

—Vonna Lovett
Breast Cancer Survivor

Jane has developed a wonderful instrument of emotional healing for women who are fighting breast cancer. Her tender questions provide the impetus for communicating thoughts, fears, worries, and prayers, while also recording the supernatural provision and faithfulness of our heavenly Father. Jane's faith, healing, and transparent dependency upon the Lord offer powerful encouragement to us all.

—Shannon Fouts
Co-pastor of North Church in Oklahoma City

a Jar *for my* Tears

a Jar *for my* Tears

JANE WILSON

A Journal Of Prayer & Healing For Women With Breast Cancer

TATE PUBLISHING *& Enterprises*

Published by Tate Publishing & Enterprises, LLC
127 E. Trade Center Terrace | Mustang, Oklahoma 73064 USA
1.888.361.9473 | www.tatepublishing.com

Tate Publishing is committed to excellence in the publishing industry. The company reflects the philosophy established by the founders, based on Psalm 68:11,
"The Lord gave the word and great was the company of those who published it."

Book design copyright © 2009 by Tate Publishing, LLC. All rights reserved.
Cover design by Kandi Evans
Interior design by Nathan Harmony

Published in the United States of America

ISBN: 978-1-60799-953-9
1. Self-Help: Stress Management: Journaling
2. Health & Fitness: Diseases: Breast Cancer
09.08.24

You keep track of all my sorrows. You have collected all my tears in your bottle. You have recorded each one in your book.

Psalm 56:8 (NLT)

Dedication

To my husband, Bill, who never allowed the laughter to die in our home. And to my beautiful daughter, Amanda, who blossomed into such a lovely young woman while tenderly caring for her sick mother.

Acknowledgments

The author expresses sincere appreciation to the follow-ing people; because of your input and support, this "God Idea" became a reality:

Stacie Jennings, you were the first person I approached with the idea for this book. Your genuine excitement and enthusi-asm about the project, coupled with sound advice, encouraged me to take the first step. You are a matchless friend.

Dr. Shirley Roddy and my fellow students at Mid-America Christian University, your encouragement of my research project gave me the deadlines that were neces-sary to complete the first draft of my book. Thank you for believing in me and allowing me to *try out* this idea.

Merillee Jesseph and Vicki Thorp, you girls sustained me during my cancer treatment in ways you will never know. And as if your friendship and physical support weren't enough, you never minded proofreading my man-uscripts and giving me your valuable input along the way. I will forever be thankful for your time, your talents, and your friendship.

To Candy Bartee, who listened to the prompting of

the Holy Spirit and fearlessly suggested a perfect title for this book. You, my friend, are one in a million.

To the multitude of friends, family, and coworkers who fed my family; bought my groceries; cleaned my house; chauffeured me to doctor appointments; did my job while I was off work; sent me cards, notes, text messages, e-mails, and phone calls of encouragement; came to see me in the hospital; and prayed for me, you were such an inspiration for this book.

Most of all, thanks to God for allowing me to dream a big dream.

Table of Contents

Foreword

J.M. Barrie, the creator of Peter Pan, once wrote "The life of every man is a diary in which he means to write one story, and writes another." Any woman who is dealing with the trauma of a breast cancer diagnosis can certainly relate to Barrie's notion of living a life that you thought was headed in one direction, but suddenly and dramatically took a turn for an entirely new one. Perhaps the most shocking thing about any serious diagnosis is not the fear or the pain, but simply the element of surprise. How can life go on with any sense of normalcy when the foundation of that life has been shaken to its very core?

Journaling is a deeply personal and very cathartic way of making sense of some of the powerful emotions that swim around you during this confusing time. A good journal can help you discover a sense of introspection that is sometimes missing from prayer alone. My sister Jane's story can serve as a series of guideposts for your own journey, as well as a reminder of God's enduring love and faithfulness. In watching Jane these past ten years since her diagnosis, I can say with some confidence that on the other side of your own diagnosis is great wisdom coupled with a sense of joy and peace like none you have ever known. The path will be arduous, but as the psalmist says, "Weeping may endure for a night, but joy comes in the morning."

—Sara Weinstock

Jane's Story

Cancer.

A word that stirs up emotions of fear and dread unlike almost any other word.

Breast Cancer.

Two words that can shake a woman to her very core and signify a loss of everything that makes her uniquely feminine.

For me, those words changed my world, and those fears became a reality.

I was diagnosed with breast cancer the Monday before Thanksgiving in 1999. Even though my husband had offered to accompany me, I was so sure that the lump in my breast was nothing to worry about, I arrived at the mammogram clinic alone. After the technician completed the mammogram and ultrasound, the doctor ordered a needle biopsy. It was painful, and I was becoming more and more frightened as the procedure wore on. After the doctor looked at the tissue sample, he said it "looked like cancer" but that he would send it off to the lab for verification. He mumbled something about "cancer not being the death sentence it once was," and I sat there in complete shock. This could not be happening to me! The doctor and technician left the room, and I began to sob. After quite a long time, the technician came back into the room to check on me. She put her arms around me and let me cry for a long, long time. Afterward, I got dressed and drove home in a daze. Normally a happy-go-lucky person, I seriously thought about driving my car into a bridge abutment. I was scared and miserable.

All the way home I remembered how sick my dad was in his final few months of life. He had died two years earlier of lung cancer, and the chemotherapy treatments completely debilitated him, making him sick and unable to function at even the lowest level. His cancer metastasized to his brain, causing him to become someone I didn't even recognize. My once strong and virile father had become slow and weak, and his memory and vocabulary functions failed him daily. I didn't want to become what I had seen him become, and I didn't want to put my family through that misery.

After I got home, I called my husband and, over the phone, blurted out those awful words, "I have cancer!" He came home immediately and just held me and let me cry.

All that afternoon and evening my head was in a fog, and I couldn't think clearly. I began to cry out to God about my physical healing, but more for my emotions. I just could not stop crying and felt like my world was spinning out of control. It was several hours later that I began to feel the Spirit of the Lord prepare my heart and my mind for the road that was before me. I really had no idea how many decisions would need to be made during the next few months, but the Spirit of the Lord began to calm my fears and help me to focus.

It was during those times of prayer that God began to stress the importance of saturating myself in Scripture. He made it clear to me that his Word would be the answer to my prayers and would provide the health that my body and emotions sought.

As I continued to seek the Lord about my healing and my emotions, I decided somehow with God's strength in my life, I would win over cancer. I purposed in my heart not to get bitter about this diagnosis. I even asked God to help me have such a good attitude during my illness that people who were not close to me would not even notice that I was experiencing this crisis in my life. It was very important to me to retain a sense of normalcy, and I was horrified that I would be thought of as a cancer patient.

After much consideration, I decided to delay the mastectomy until my daughter's Christmas break from college. I didn't want her to be concerned about me during finals, and selfishly wanted her to be home with me while I recuperated. I was scheduled to have a partial mastectomy on December 22. The surgeon determined that only about 10 percent of my right breast would need to be removed—a lumpectomy. We discussed at length how routine this surgery would be, and my prognosis looked very good. At this point in time, they thought the cancer was stage 1 and that, depending on the lab results, I might not even need chemotherapy, only localized radiation treatments. I even asked the doctor what the chances were that he had made a mistake and that I would need a complete mastectomy.

"That has only happened to me once," he said. Even so, somewhere inside I felt uneasy and wasn't confident of the surgical outcome. I asked God to give me the strength to face the surgery with grace and dignity.

At this time, I was still in shock, afraid, and very emotional. I didn't want "the general public" to know what I was going through. Even though I usually was a very "what you see is what you get" kind of person, I only told my close friends and family and closely guarded my privacy. I was hoping against hope that the mastectomy would be the end of it. But the moment I woke up from surgery, I knew that something was wrong. I was in extreme pain and lifted the surgical blanket off my breast. Then I saw that over 60 percent of my breast was gone, including the nipple. Alone in the recovery room, I began to sob.

That evening, the surgeon came into my hospital room to tell me news that, to this day, I don't think ever soaked in. The tumor was three to four times larger than he thought. Additionally, he had removed over twenty-five lymph nodes and *each one* tested positive for cancer. That meant the cancer was beginning to spread. How far, he didn't know. He had scheduled a battery of tests for the next morning and wanted me to spend the night in the hospital. I sat there in disbelief as he told me how bad things really could be. If the cancer had spread to organs or bones, my treatment options would be very limited, as well as my days on earth.

The next morning I had a CAT scan, an MRI, and a bone scan. Thankfully, each one was negative, but the large number of positive lymph nodes was still a great concern. The diagnosis had gone from stage 1 to stage 3b. Chemotherapy and radiation treatments would have to begin immediately. My surgeon was very emphatic when he said, "Jane, you *must* do everything that is available to you to treat this! We have to buy you some time!" I just couldn't comprehend it. How could I have cancer, and how could it have spread so far without my knowledge?

While the rest of the world was ringing in the new millennium, I was planning my cancer treatment. The first week of January was spent at the oncologist's office, and I had my first round of chemo only three weeks after surgery. Things were moving so fast! After my second round of chemo, my oncologist suggested that I see a specialist about having a stem cell transplant coupled with high dose chemotherapy, an extremely risky procedure that would mean a solid month of treatment.

At each stage of my treatment (mastectomy, chemo, stem cell transplant, radiation, and reconstruction), I began to see how God only took me as far as the next step but never beyond. I kept trying to look at the whole picture, to formulate a long-range plan and make decisions line up like dominoes in a row. But God had different plans for me. At each major fork in the road, it seemed I could only plan the next step and no further. After a while, I began to see God's timing in the decision-making process and began to rest in his divine guidance. I kept asking him to be in control but stupidly kept trying to guide the process anyway. It was only after I let go and turned everything over to him that I began to have true peace. Even though I was scared, when I quieted the voices in my head and listened to my heart, I was at peace with my decisions. The best way I can describe it is to say that deep down inside—where *I am who I am,* and God *reveals to me who he is*—I was at peace, and I knew that God was guiding my footsteps.

The stem cell transplant with high dose chemo was grueling. But, as predicted by a seasoned oncology nurse, the process would "seem like a dream" afterward. Thankfully, she was right. Of course, I remember the four weeks I received daily treatment, but it does seem like a blur. I felt so awful that I slept for hours and hours each day. But I can truthfully say God was with me every hour of every day. I breezed through the treatment with almost no complications. My white blood counts bounced back, and my strength was back to normal in just a few months' time.

I was forty years old when I was diagnosed in 1999. I have always been a planner by nature, and I enjoy plotting even the smallest details of life. So after I was diagnosed, I began to reluctantly revise my plans for the future. Even though the cancer had spread to my lymph nodes, I felt sure that even in the worst-case scenario I would live another two or three years. What a wonderful blessing my forty-fifth birthday was because it was the first birthday that I wasn't sure I was going to have! In 1999, my oncologist did not promise that I would see the year 2004. And as I write this, my fiftieth birthday has been celebrated—a real milestone in more ways than one. I will *never* dread another birthday or hide my age from anyone. God is so wonderful to give us milestones to celebrate with our friends and family. I look forward to each and every year that he gives me with great anticipation and true thankfulness. I can't wait to celebrate many, many more birthdays with my husband, daughter, and future grandchildren.

My current state of health is great, and I feel healed and whole, with only my scars as a reminder of the ordeal I went through. I am able to do whatever I please, my stamina is terrific, and my blood counts are back to normal. Praise God for his faithfulness. I will never be the same again.

May the blessings of God be revealed to you during this unique time in your life,

—Jane

> You turned my wailing into dancing; you removed my sackcloth and clothed me with joy, that my heart may sing to you and not be silent. O Lord my God, I will give you thanks forever.
>
> Psalm 30:11–12

A Jar for My Tears: The Journal

A gift for you

Joanie Writing and reading helps to heal your soul. It worked for me. I am thinking of you everyday and I admire your courage. Hang in there. Love Donna.

After my cancer treatment was completed, I decided to return to college and finish my degree. Life and work obligations had prevented me from finishing when I was younger, and my recent diagnosis had drawn attention to the uncompleted goals in my life. It was during this time that God gave me the idea of creating this journal of prayer and healing for women with breast cancer. I began to research the benefits of journaling, prayer, and meditation during breast cancer treatment. My research overwhelmingly supported what God had spoken to me months earlier: that his Word coupled with journaling and prayer would greatly reduce stress, help a breast cancer patient cope, improve her prognosis, and help alleviate her depression. As a result of that research project, this journal was born.

If you've recently been diagnosed with cancer, I understand how you're feeling right now. But more importantly, God knows how you are feeling too. Please know that he is your *healer* and your *strength*. I want to encourage you to get past the shock and denial and move toward God's healing for your body, mind, and emotions.

"A jar for my tears" is a lovely metaphor for the act of journaling all your worries, thoughts, complaints, fears, and prayers. By writing down your concerns, you are facing them square in the eye—not running scared. Be open and honest with yourself and with God. No one will see this journal but you. By writing in your journal, you symbolically place your tears in this jar and turn your concerns over to God. "Give all your worries and cares to God, for he cares about you" (1 Peter 5:7, NLT). Know that he hears your prayers and hurries to answer them.

The journal is divided into sections, beginning with your diagnosis, continuing on through your surgery, chemotherapy and radiation treatments, and ending with your breast reconstruction. Use whatever portions of the journal apply to your situation. After each section, there is a page called *My Secret Place*. Use this page to track the changes in your emotions and concerns. During this journey, you'll see how God is moving in your life and in the lives of those around you.

Remember, this is only a season in your life. Cancer does not define who you are. You are a woman, wife, mother, volunteer, church member, employee or employer, and much, much more. But most of all, you are a daughter of the Most High God.

> But let all who take refuge in you be glad; let them ever sing for joy.
>
> Psalm 5:11

My Diagnosis and Treatment

My Diagnosis

What emotions do I feel? Am I afraid, sad, angry, anxious, ashamed?

_____

_____

_____

_____

_____

_____

_____

_____

_____

_____

_____

_____

For the Lord watches over the way of the righteous.

Psalm 1:6a

So do not fear, for I am with you; do not be dismayed, for I am your God. I will strengthen you and help you; I will uphold you with my righteous right hand. All who rage against you will surely be ashamed and disgraced; those who oppose you will be as nothing and perish. Though you search for your enemies, you will not find them. Those who wage war against you will be as nothing at all. For I am the Lord, your God, who takes hold of your right hand and says to you, "Do not fear; I will help you. Do not be afraid … for I myself will help you …" declares the Lord, your Redeemer.

Isaiah 41:10–14

My Secret Place

My greatest fears are:

_____

_____

_____

_____

_____

My greatest desires are:

_____

_____

_____

_____

_____

My greatest hopes are:

_____

_____

_____

_____

_____

My favorite scriptures are:

_____

_____

_____

_____

_____

Today's date: _____

My Concerns

I would describe my concerns for myself, my family, my friends, my coworkers as...

_____

_____

_____

_____

_____

_____

_____

_____

_____

_____

_____

_____

_____

_____

With whom will I share this information? How will I tell them? Is there anyone I do not want to share my diagnosis with?

_____

_____

_____

_____

_____

_____

_____

The Lord is my shepherd, I shall lack nothing. He makes me lie down in green pastures, he leads me beside quiet waters, he restores my soul. He guides me in paths of righteousness for his name's sake. Even though I walk through the valley of the shadow of death, I will fear no evil, for you are with me; your rod and your staff, they comfort me. You prepare a table before me in the presence of my enemies. You anoint my head with oil; my cup overflows. Surely goodness and love will follow me all the days of my life, and I will dwell in the house of the Lord forever.

Psalm 23:1–6

I would describe my feelings about joining a support group or contacting a counselor or therapist as ...

_____

_____

_____

_____

_____

_____

_____

_____

_____

_____

_____

_____

_____

I love you, O Lord, my strength. The Lord is my rock, my fortress and my deliverer; my God is my rock, in whom I take refuge. He is my shield and the horn of my salvation, my stronghold. I call to the Lord, who is worthy of praise, and I am saved from my enemies. The cords of death entangled me; the torrents of destruction overwhelmed me. The cords of the grave coiled around me; the snares of death confronted me. In my distress I called to the Lord; I cried to my God for help. From his temple he heard my voice; my cry came before him, into his ears ... He reached down from on high and took hold of me; he drew me out of deep waters. He rescued me from my powerful enemy, from my foes, who were too strong for me. They confronted me in the day of my disaster, but the Lord was my support. He brought me out into a spacious place; he rescued me because he delighted in me.

Psalm 18:1–6; 16–19

My Secret Place

My greatest fears are:

_____

_____

_____

_____

_____

My greatest desires are:

_____

_____

_____

_____

_____

My greatest hopes are:

_____

_____

_____

_____

_____

My favorite scriptures are:

_____

_____

_____

_____

_____

Today's date: _____

My Treatment Decisions

I would describe my concerns about surgery, chemotherapy, radiation, and breast reconstruction as ...

_____

_____

_____

_____

_____

_____

_____

_____

_____

_____

_____

_____

_____

_____

Do I have a choice between a mastectomy and a lumpectomy? I would describe my feelings about my choice as…

_____

_____

_____

_____

_____

_____

_____

_____

_____

For the Lord gives wisdom, and from his mouth come knowledge and understanding. He holds victory in store for the upright, he is a shield to those whose walk is blameless, for he guards the course of the just and protects the way of his faithful ones.

Proverbs 2:6–8

Have I openly discussed my concerns with my husband and children? What are their concerns?

_____

_____

_____

_____

_____

_____

_____

_____

_____

_____

_____

_____

_____

Have we discussed who will take care of me and my family while I recuperate?

_____

_____

_____

_____

_____

_____

_____

_____

My daughter, preserve sound judgment and discernment, do not let them out of your sight; they will be life for you, an ornament to grace your neck. Then you will go on your way in safety, and your foot will not stumble; when you lie down, you will not be afraid; when you lie down, your sleep will be sweet. Have no fear of sudden disaster or of the ruin that overtakes the wicked, for the Lord will be your confidence and will keep your foot from being snared.

Proverbs 3:21–26

My Secret Place

My greatest fears are:

_____

_____

_____

_____

_____

My greatest desires are:

_____

_____

_____

_____

_____

My greatest hopes are:

_____

_____

_____

_____

_____

_____

My favorite scriptures are:

_____

_____

_____

_____

_____

_____

Today's date: _____

After Surgery

How do I feel physically, emotionally, spiritually? How have I been coping with my new body?

_____

_____

_____

_____

_____

_____

_____

_____

_____

_____

_____

_____

_____

_____

Was the surgery a success? What is my prognosis?

_____

_____

_____

_____

_____

_____

_____

_____

_____

_____

_____

Guard my life and rescue me ... for I take refuge
in you.

Psalm 25:20

What further treatment has been recommended for me? How do I feel about my doctor's recommendations?

_____

_____

_____

_____

_____

_____

_____

_____

_____

_____

_____

_____

_____

_____

Spread your protection over them, that those who love your name may rejoice in you. For surely, O Lord, you bless the righteous; you surround them with your favor as with a shield.

Psalm 5:11b-12

My Secret Place

My greatest fears are:

_____

_____

_____

_____

_____

My greatest desires are:

_____

_____

_____

_____

_____

My greatest hopes are:

_____

_____

_____

_____

_____

My favorite scriptures are:

_____

_____

_____

_____

_____

Today's date: _____

My First
Chemotherapy
Treatment

What are my emotions? What are my concerns? How do I feel physically? Spiritually? Mentally?

_____

_____

_____

_____

_____

_____

_____

_____

_____

_____

_____

_____

_____

How am I coping? How do I feel when I am alone with my thoughts?

_____

_____

_____

_____

_____

_____

_____

_____

_____

_____

_____

> Keep me safe, O God, for in you I take refuge. I said to the Lord, "You are my Lord; apart from you I have no good thing."
>
> Psalm 16:1–2

How do I feel about the possibility of losing my hair?

_____

_____

_____

_____

_____

_____

_____

_____

_____

_____

_____

_____

_____

_____

What are my questions for my doctor?

_____

_____

_____

_____

_____

_____

_____

_____

_____

_____

_____

May the words of my mouth and the meditation
of my heart be pleasing in your sight, O Lord, my
Rock and my Redeemer.

Psalm 19:14

My Secret Place

My greatest fears are:

_____

_____

_____

_____

_____

My greatest desires are:

_____

_____

_____

_____

_____

_____

My greatest hopes are:

_____

_____

_____

_____

_____

_____

My favorite scriptures are:

_____

_____

_____

_____

_____

_____

Today's date: _____

After My First

Chemotherapy

Treatment

How do I feel physically? Am I weak, nauseated, dizzy, or fatigued?

_____

_____

_____

_____

_____

_____

_____

_____

_____

_____

_____

_____

_____

How am I coping? How do I feel when I am alone with my thoughts?

_____

_____

_____

_____

_____

_____

_____

_____

_____

_____

_____

Answer me when I call to you, O my righteous God. Give me relief from my distress; be merciful to me and hear my prayer.

Psalm 4:1

Am I having difficulty sleeping?

_____

_____

_____

_____

_____

_____

_____

_____

_____

_____

_____

_____

_____

What are my questions for my doctor?

_____

_____

_____

_____

_____

_____

_____

_____

_____

_____

The Lord is close to the brokenhearted and saves those who are crushed in spirit. A righteous woman may have many troubles, but the Lord delivers her from them all.

Psalm 34:18–19

My Secret Place

My greatest fears are:

_____

_____

_____

_____

_____

My greatest desires are:

_____

_____

_____

_____

_____

My greatest hopes are:

_____

_____

_____

_____

_____

My favorite scriptures are:

_____

_____

_____

_____

_____

Today's date: _____

Additional Chemotherapy Treatment Days

Today's date: _____

What are my emotions? What are my concerns? How do
I feel physically? Spiritually? Mentally?

_____

_____

_____

_____

_____

_____

_____

_____

_____

_____

_____

_____

_____

_____

How am I coping? How do I feel when I am alone with my thoughts?

_____

_____

_____

_____

_____

_____

_____

_____

_____

_____

The angel of the Lord encamps around those who fear him, and he delivers them. Taste and see that the Lord is good; blessed is the woman who takes refuge in him.

Psalm 34:7–8

Am I having difficulty sleeping? Eating?

What are my questions for my doctor?

_____

_____

_____

_____

_____

_____

_____

_____

_____

_____

_____

_____

He does not ignore the cry of the afflicted.

Psalm 9:12b

Additional Chemotherapy Treatment Days

Today's date: _____

What are my emotions? What are my concerns? How do I feel physically? Spiritually? Mentally?

_____

_____

_____

_____

_____

_____

_____

_____

_____

_____

_____

How am I coping? How do I feel when I am alone with my thoughts?

_____

_____

_____

_____

_____

_____

_____

_____

_____

_____

_____

According to your love remember me, for you are good, O Lord.

Psalm 25:7b

Am I having difficulty sleeping? Eating?

_____

_____

_____

_____

_____

_____

_____

_____

_____

_____

_____

_____

_____

What are my questions for my doctor?

_____

_____

_____

_____

_____

_____

_____

_____

_____

_____

I will lie down and sleep in peace, for you alone, O
Lord, make me dwell in safety.

Psalm 4:8

Additional Chemotherapy Treatment Days

Today's date: _____

What are my emotions? What are my concerns? How do I feel physically? Spiritually? Mentally?

_____

_____

_____

_____

_____

_____

_____

_____

_____

_____

_____

_____

How am I coping? How do I feel when I am alone with my thoughts?

_____

_____

_____

_____

_____

_____

_____

_____

_____

_____

Blessed is the woman who finds wisdom, the woman who gains understanding, for she [wisdom] is more profitable than silver and yields better returns than gold. She [wisdom] is more precious than rubies; nothing you desire can compare with her.

Proverbs 3:13–15

Am I having difficulty sleeping? Eating?

_____

_____

_____

_____

_____

_____

_____

_____

_____

_____

_____

_____

_____

_____

What are my questions for my doctor?

_____

_____

_____

_____

_____

_____

_____

_____

_____

_____

I will praise the Lord, who counsels me; even at night my heart instructs me. I have set the Lord always before me. Because he is at my right hand, I will not be shaken. Therefore, my heart is glad and my tongue rejoices; my body also will rest secure, because you will not abandon me to the grave.

Psalm 16:7–10

Additional Chemotherapy Treatment Days

Today's date: _____

What are my emotions? What are my concerns? How do I feel physically? Spiritually? Mentally?

_____

_____

_____

_____

_____

_____

_____

_____

_____

_____

_____

_____

How am I coping? How do I feel when I am alone with
my thoughts?

_____

_____

_____

_____

_____

_____

_____

_____

_____

_____

_____

For the Lord watches over the way of the righteous.
Psalm 1:6

Am I having difficulty sleeping? Eating?

_____

_____

_____

_____

_____

_____

_____

_____

_____

_____

_____

_____

_____

_____

What are my questions for my doctor?

_____

_____

_____

_____

_____

_____

_____

_____

_____

Blessed is the woman who does not walk in the
counsel of the wicked, or stand in the way of sinners,
or sit in the seat of mockers. But her delight is in
the law of the Lord, and on his law she meditates
day and night. She is like a tree planted by streams
of water, which yields its fruit in season and whose
leaf does not wither. Whatever she does prospers.

Psalm 1:1–3

My Secret Place

My greatest fears are:

_____

_____

_____

_____

_____

My greatest desires are:

_____

_____

_____

_____

_____

My greatest hopes are:

_____

_____

_____

_____

_____

_____

My favorite scriptures are:

_____

_____

_____

_____

_____

_____

Today's date: _____

After Chemotherapy Treatment Is Over

Was there a particular person who helped me or my family during my treatment? How did his or her help make me feel? Have I expressed my thanks to that person?

_____

_____

_____

_____

_____

_____

_____

_____

_____

_____

_____

_____

What do I plan to do to help others in a similar way in the future?

_____

_____

_____

_____

_____

_____

_____

_____

_____

_____

_____

_____

_____

How am I coping? How do I feel when I am alone with my thoughts?

_____

_____

_____

_____

_____

_____

_____

_____

_____

_____

_____

_____

> You hear, O Lord, the desire of the afflicted; you
> encourage them, and you listen to their cry.
>
> Psalm 10:17

What are my questions for my doctor?

_____

_____

_____

_____

_____

_____

_____

_____

_____

Be merciful to me, Lord, for I am faint; O Lord, heal me, for my bones are in agony. My soul is in anguish. How long, O Lord, how long? Turn, O Lord, and deliver me; save me because of your unfailing love.

Psalm 6:2–4

My Secret Place

My greatest fears are:

_____

_____

_____

_____

_____

My greatest desires are:

_____

_____

_____

_____

_____

My greatest hopes are:

_____

_____

_____

_____

_____

My favorite scriptures are:

_____

_____

_____

_____

_____

_____

Today's date: _____

Radiation Treatments

Today's date: _____

How are my radiation treatments going? Am I fatigued?

_____

_____

_____

_____

_____

_____

_____

_____

_____

_____

_____

_____

_____

How am I coping?

_____

_____

_____

_____

_____

_____

_____

_____

_____

_____

_____

_____

_____

_____

What are my questions for my doctor?

_____

_____

_____

_____

_____

_____

_____

_____

_____

_____

_____

> The Lord has heard my cry for mercy; the Lord accepts my prayer. May all my enemies be ashamed and dismayed; may they turn back in sudden disgrace.
>
> Psalm 6:9–10

Radiation Treatments

Today's date: _____

How are my radiation treatments going? Am I fatigued?

_____

_____

_____

_____

_____

_____

_____

_____

_____

_____

_____

_____

How am I coping?

_____

_____

_____

_____

_____

_____

_____

_____

_____

_____

_____

_____

_____

What are my questions for my doctor?

But I trust in your unfailing love; my heart rejoices in your salvation. I will sing to the Lord, for he has been good to me.

Psalm 13:5–6

Radiation Treatments

Today's date: _____

How are my radiation treatments going? Am I fatigued?

_____

_____

_____

_____

_____

_____

_____

_____

_____

_____

_____

_____

How am I coping?

_____

_____

_____

_____

_____

_____

_____

_____

_____

_____

_____

_____

_____

_____

What are my questions for my doctor?

_____

_____

_____

_____

_____

_____

_____

_____

_____

_____

> Praise be to the Lord, for he has heard my cry for mercy. The Lord is my strength and my shield; my heart trusts in him, and I am helped. My heart leaps for joy and I will give thanks to him in song. The Lord is the strength of his people, a fortress of salvation for his anointed one.
>
> Psalm 28:6–8

Radiation Treatments

Today's date: _____

How are my radiation treatments going? Am I fatigued?

_____

_____

_____

_____

_____

_____

_____

_____

_____

_____

_____

_____

_____

How am I coping?

_____

_____

_____

_____

_____

_____

_____

_____

_____

_____

_____

_____

_____

What are my questions for my doctor?

_____

_____

_____

_____

_____

_____

_____

_____

_____

_____

_____

Keep me as the apple of your eye; hide me in the
shadow of your wings from the wicked who assail
me, from my mortal enemies who surround me.

Psalm 17:8–9

Radiation Treatments

Today's date: _____

How are my radiation treatments going? Am I fatigued?

_____

_____

_____

_____

_____

_____

_____

_____

_____

_____

_____

_____

_____

How am I coping?

_____

_____

_____

_____

_____

_____

_____

_____

_____

_____

_____

_____

What are my questions for my doctor?

_____

_____

_____

_____

_____

_____

_____

_____

_____

_____

My shield is God Most High, who saves the
upright in heart.

Psalm 7:10

Radiation Treatments

Today's date: _____

How are my radiation treatments going? Am I fatigued?

_____

_____

_____

_____

_____

_____

_____

_____

_____

_____

_____

_____

How am I coping?

_____

_____

_____

_____

_____

_____

_____

_____

_____

_____

_____

_____

_____

What are my questions for my doctor?

_____

_____

_____

_____

_____

_____

_____

_____

_____

_____

_____

Do not be wise in your own eyes; fear the Lord and shun evil. This will bring health to your body and nourishment to your bones.

Proverbs 3:7–8

My Secret Place

My greatest fears are:

_____

_____

_____

_____

_____

My greatest desires are:

_____

_____

_____

_____

_____

My greatest hopes are:

_____

_____

_____

_____

_____

My favorite scriptures are:

_____

_____

_____

_____

_____

_____

Today's date: _____

Breast Reconstruction

What are my options for breast reconstruction?

_____

_____

_____

_____

_____

_____

_____

_____

_____

_____

_____

_____

_____

How do I feel about my body? How would reconstructive surgery make me feel differently about myself?

_____

_____

_____

_____

_____

_____

_____

_____

_____

_____

Long life is in her [wisdom's] right hand; in her left hand are riches and honor. Her ways are pleasant ways, and all her paths are peace. She is a tree of life to those who embrace her; those who lay hold of her will be blessed.

Proverbs 3:16–18

What are my questions for my doctor?

I am still confident of this: I will see the goodness of the Lord in the land of the living. Wait for the Lord; be strong and take heart and wait for the Lord.

Psalm 27:13–14

My Secret Place

My greatest fears are:

_____

_____

_____

_____

_____

My greatest desires are:

_____

_____

_____

_____

_____

My greatest hopes are:

_____

_____

_____

_____

_____

_____

My favorite scriptures are:

_____

_____

_____

_____

_____

_____

Today's date: _____

Relationships with Those I Love

Changes in Me

What has changed about me since this journey began?

_____

_____

_____

_____

_____

_____

_____

_____

_____

_____

_____

_____

_____

Who has been the most help to me? How have they shown me love?

_____

_____

_____

_____

_____

_____

_____

_____

_____

I will exalt You, O Lord, for you lifted me out of the depths and did not let my enemies gloat over me. O Lord my God, I called to you for help and you healed me. O Lord, you brought me up from the grave; you spared me from going down into the pit.

Psalm 30:1–3

My Secret Place

My greatest fears are:

_____

_____

_____

_____

_____

_____

My greatest desires are:

_____

_____

_____

_____

_____

_____

My greatest hopes are:

_____

_____

_____

_____

_____

My favorite scriptures are:

_____

_____

_____

_____

_____

Today's date: _____

Changes in My Family

Has my husband been able to express his concerns to me?
Have we grown closer together during this time?

_____

_____

_____

_____

_____

_____

_____

_____

_____

_____

_____

_____

_____

What about my children?

_____

_____

_____

_____

_____

_____

_____

_____

_____

_____

_____

I will give thanks to the Lord because of his righteousness and will sing praise to the name of the Lord Most High.

Psalm 7:17

My Secret Place

My greatest fears are:

_____

_____

_____

_____

_____

My greatest desires are:

_____

_____

_____

_____

_____

My greatest hopes are:

_____

_____

_____

_____

_____

_____

My favorite scriptures are:

_____

_____

_____

_____

_____

_____

Today's date: _____

Changes in My Emotions

Have I found it difficult to discuss my fears or concerns with my husband or family?

_____

_____

_____

_____

_____

_____

_____

_____

_____

_____

_____

_____

Do I feel any unresolved anger—toward God, myself, or others?

_____

_____

_____

_____

_____

_____

_____

_____

_____

But the eyes of the Lord are on those who fear him, on those whose hope is in his unfailing love, to deliver them from death and keep them alive in famine. We wait in hope for the Lord; he is our help and our shield. In him our hearts rejoice, for we trust in his holy name. May your unfailing love rest upon us, O Lord, even as we put our hope in you.

Psalm 33:18–22

My Secret Place

My greatest fears are:

_____

_____

_____

_____

_____

_____

My greatest desires are:

_____

_____

_____

_____

_____

_____

My greatest hopes are:

_____

_____

_____

_____

_____

_____

My favorite scriptures are:

_____

_____

_____

_____

_____

_____

Today's date: _____

My Future

Life, Death, and Eternity

How has this experience changed my views of life and death? Of eternity?

_____

_____

_____

_____

_____

_____

_____

_____

_____

_____

_____

_____

_____

_____

_____

_____

_____

_____

_____

_____

_____

_____

_____

_____

_____

For through me your days will be many, and years
will be added to your life.

Proverbs 9:11

My Secret Place

My greatest fears are:

_____

_____

_____

_____

_____

My greatest desires are:

_____

_____

_____

_____

_____

My greatest hopes are:

_____

_____

_____

_____

_____

_____

My favorite scriptures are:

_____

_____

_____

_____

_____

_____

Today's date: _____

My Goals and Plans

Did I promise myself my life would be different after this experience? Did I set any goals for myself? Have my plans changed?

_____

_____

_____

_____

_____

_____

_____

_____

_____

_____

_____

_____

_____

_____

_____

_____

_____

_____

_____

_____

_____

_____

I sought the Lord, and he answered me; he
delivered me from all my fears.

Psalm 34:4

Being confident of this, that he who began a good
work in you will carry it on to completion until the
day of Christ Jesus.

Philippians 1:6

My Secret Place

My greatest fears are:

_____

_____

_____

_____

_____

My greatest desires are:

_____

_____

_____

_____

_____

My greatest hopes are:

_____

_____

_____

_____

_____

My favorite scriptures are:

_____

_____

_____

_____

_____

Today's date: _____

What I've Learned on This Journey

What have I learned through this experience?

_____

_____

_____

_____

_____

_____

_____

_____

_____

_____

_____

_____

_____

How do I feel about sharing that knowledge with others?

_____

_____

_____

_____

_____

_____

_____

_____

_____

_____

I will praise you, O Lord, with all my heart; I will tell of all your wonders. I will be glad and rejoice in you; I will sing praise to your name, O Most High. My enemies turn back; they stumble and perish before you. For you have upheld my right and my cause.

Psalm 9:1–4a

My Secret Place

My greatest fears are:

_____

_____

_____

_____

_____

My greatest desires are:

_____

_____

_____

_____

_____

My greatest hopes are:

_____

_____

_____

_____

_____

My favorite scriptures are:

_____

_____

_____

_____

_____

_____

Today's date: _____

As I Pour
Out My Jar

My Prayers of Petition

My Prayers of Petition

(asking for something for myself)

_____

_____

_____

_____

_____

_____

_____

_____

_____

_____

_____

_____

_____

_____

_____

_____

_____

_____

_____

_____

_____

_____

_____

_____

_____

_____

_____

_____

_____

_____

_____

_____

_____

_____

_____

_____

_____

_____

_____

_____

_____

_____

_____

In my distress I called to the Lord; I cried to my
God for help. From his temple he heard my voice;
my cry came before him, into his ears.

Psalm 18:6

My Prayers of
Intercession

My Prayers of Intercession

(asking something for others)

_____

_____

_____

_____

_____

_____

_____

_____

_____

_____

_____

_____

_____

_____

_____

_____

_____

_____

_____

_____

_____

_____

_____

_____

_____

_____

_____

_____

_____

_____

_____

_____

_____

_____

_____

_____

_____

_____

_____

_____

_____

_____

I urge, then, first of all, that requests, prayers, intercession and thanksgiving be made for everyone.

1 Timothy 2:1

My Prayers of
Confession

My Prayers of Confession

(expressing repentance of wrongdoing and asking forgiveness)

_____

_____

_____

_____

_____

_____

_____

_____

_____

_____

_____

_____

_____

Repent, then, and turn to God, so that your sins
may be wiped out, that times of refreshing may
come from the Lord.

Acts 3:19a

My Prayers of
Lamentation

My Prayers of Lamentation

(crying out in distress and asking for vindication)

_____

_____

_____

_____

_____

_____

_____

_____

_____

_____

_____

_____

_____

_____

_____

_____

_____

_____

_____

_____

_____

_____

_____

_____

_____

_____

Turn to me and be gracious to me, for I am lonely and afflicted. The troubles of my heart have multiplied; free me from my anguish. Look upon my affliction and my distress and take away all my sins.

Psalm 25:16–18

My Prayers of
Adoration

My Prayers of Adoration

(giving honor and praise)

_____

_____

_____

_____

_____

_____

_____

_____

_____

_____

_____

_____

_____

I will praise God's name in song and glorify him
with thanksgiving.

Psalm 69:30

My Prayers of
Invocation

My Prayers of Invocation

(summoning the presence of God)

_____

_____

_____

_____

_____

_____

_____

_____

_____

_____

_____

_____

_____

_____

_____

_____

_____

_____

_____

_____

_____

_____

_____

_____

_____

_____

You have made known to me the path of life; you
will fill me with joy in your presence, with eternal
pleasures at your right hand.

Psalm 16:11

My Prayers of
Thanksgiving

My Prayers of Thanksgiving

(offering gratitude)

_____

_____

_____

_____

_____

_____

_____

_____

_____

_____

_____

_____

_____

_____

_____

_____

_____

_____

_____

_____

_____

_____

_____

_____

_____

_____

_____

_____

_____

_____

_____

_____

_____

_____

_____

_____

_____

_____

_____

_____

_____

_____

_____

The Lord is my strength and my shield; my heart trusts in him, and I am helped. My heart leaps for joy and I will give thanks to him in song.

Psalm 28:7

More Scriptures

In all these things we are more than conquerors through him who loved us.

Romans 8:37

But thanks be to God! He gives us the victory through our Lord Jesus Christ.

1 Corinthians 15:57

Peace I leave with you; my peace I give you. I do not give to you as the world gives. Do not let your hearts be troubled and do not be afraid.

John 14:27

Cast all your anxiety on him because he cares for you.

1 Peter 5:7

A cheerful heart is good medicine, but a crushed spirit dries up the bones.

Proverbs 17:22

But those who hope in the Lord will renew their strength. They will soar on wings like eagles; they will run and not grow weary, they will walk and not be faint.

Isaiah 40:31

Even to your old age and gray hairs I am he, I am he who will sustain you. I have made you and I will carry you; I will sustain you and I will rescue you.

Isaiah 46:4

The thief comes only to steal and kill and destroy; I have come that they may have life, and have it to the full.

John 10:10

Do not grieve, for the joy of the Lord is your strength.

Nehemiah 8:10b

Let the redeemed of the Lord say this—those he redeemed from the hand of the foe...Let them give thanks to the Lord for his unfailing love and his wonderful deeds.

Psalm 107:2, 8

He satisfies my desires with good things so that my youth is renewed like the eagle's.

Psalm 103:5

He who did not spare his own Son, but gave him up for us all—how will he not also, along with him, graciously give us all things?

Romans 8:32

He himself bore our sins in his body on the tree, so that we might die to sins and live for righteousness; by his wounds you have been healed.

1 Peter 2:24

He sent forth his word and healed them; he rescued them from the grave.

Psalm 107:20

This is the assurance we have in approaching God: that if we ask anything according to his will, he hears us. And if we know that he hears us—whatever we ask—we know that we have what we asked of him.

1 John 5:14–15

For God so loved the world that he gave his one and only Son, that whoever believes in him shall not perish but have eternal life.

John 3:16

My purpose is that they may be encouraged in heart and united in love, so that they may have the full riches of complete understanding, in order that they may know the mystery of God, namely, Christ, in whom are hidden all the treasures of wisdom and knowledge.

Colossians 2:2–3

The fear of the Lord is the beginning of knowledge.

Proverbs 1:7a

O Lord, how many are my foes! How many rise up against me! Many are saying of me, "God will not deliver her." But you are a shield around me, O Lord, my Glorious One, who lifts up my head. To the Lord I cry aloud, and he answers me from his holy hill. I lie down and sleep; I wake again, because the Lord sustains me. I will not fear the tens of thousands drawn up against me on every side. Arise, O Lord! Deliver me, O my God! For you have struck all my enemies on the jaw; you have broken the teeth of the wicked. From the Lord comes deliverance. May your blessing be on your people.

Psalm 3:1–8

The Lord is a refuge for the oppressed, a stronghold in times of trouble. Those who know your name will trust in you, for you, Lord, have never forsaken those who seek you.

Psalm 9:9–10

O Lord, see how my enemies persecute me! Have mercy and lift me up from the gates of death, that I may declare your praises.

Psalm 9:13–14a

Let love and faithfulness never leave you; bind them around your neck, write them on the tablet of your heart. Then you will win favor and a good name in the sight of God and man. Trust in the Lord with all your heart and lean not on your own understanding; in all your ways acknowledge him, and he will make your paths straight.

Proverbs 3:3–6

Honor the Lord with your wealth, with the first fruits of all your crops; then your barns will be filled to overflowing, and your vats will brim over with new wine.

Proverbs 3:9–10

As for God, his way is perfect; the word of the Lord is flawless. He is a shield for all who take refuge in him. For who is God besides the Lord? And who is the Rock except our God?

Psalm 18:30–31

Praise be to the Lord, for he showed his wonderful love to me when I was in a besieged city. In my alarm I said, "I am cut off from your sight!" Yet you heard my cry for mercy when I called to you for help.

Psalm 31:21–22

For in the day of trouble he will keep me safe in his dwelling; he will hide me in the shelter of his tabernacle and set me high upon a rock. Then my head will be exalted above the enemies who surround me; at his tabernacle will I sacrifice with shouts of joy; I will sing and make music to the Lord.

Psalm 27:5–6

Contend, O Lord, with those who contend with me; fight against those who fight against me. Take up shield and buckler; arise and come to my aid. Brandish spear and javelin against those who pursue me. Say to my soul, "I am your salvation." May those who seek my life be disgraced and put to shame; may those who plot my ruin be turned back in dismay. May they be like chaff before the wind, with the angel of the Lord driving them away; may their path be dark and slippery, with the angel of the Lord pursuing them. Since they hid their net for me without cause and without cause dug a pit for me, may ruin overtake them by surprise—may the net they hid entangle them, may they fall into the pit, to their ruin. Then my soul will rejoice in the Lord and delight in his salvation. My whole being will exclaim, "Who is like you, O Lord?"

Psalm 35:1–10a

The Spirit helps us in our weakness. We do not know what we ought to pray, but the Spirit himself intercedes for us with groans that words cannot express. And he who searches our hearts knows the mind of the Spirit, because the Spirit intercedes for the saints in accordance with God's will.

Romans 8:26

And pray in the Spirit on all occasions with all kinds of prayers and requests. With this in mind, be alert and always keep on praying for all the saints.

Ephesians 6:18

Therefore he [Jesus] is able to save completely those who come to God through him, because he always lives to intercede for them.

Hebrews 7:25

God is our refuge and strength, an ever present help in trouble. Therefore we will not fear.

Psalm 46:1a

For God did not give us a spirit of timidity, but a spirit of power, of love and of self-discipline.

2 Timothy 1:7

This is how we know what love is: Jesus Christ laid down his life for us … This then is how we know that we belong to the truth, and how we set our hearts at rest in his presence whenever our hearts condemn us. For God is greater than our hearts, and he knows everything. Dear friends, if our hearts do not condemn us, we have confidence before God and receive from him anything we ask, because we obey his commands and do what pleases him.

1 John 3:16a; 19–22

The Spirit of the Sovereign Lord is on me, because the Lord has anointed me to preach the good news to the poor. He has sent me to bind up the brokenhearted, to proclaim freedom for the captives and release for the prisoners, to proclaim the year of the Lord's favor and the day of vengeance of our God, to comfort all who mourn, and provide for those who grieve in Zion—to bestow on them a crown of beauty instead of ashes, the oil of gladness instead of mourning, and a garment of praise instead of a spirit of despair. They will be called oaks of righteousness, a planting of the Lord for the display of his splendor.

Isaiah 61:1–3

Notes

A Final Note

As a Christian woman who has been diagnosed with breast cancer and lived through the experience, never forget that *you are not alone.* We are never alone. We always have God and his Holy Spirit to comfort us when we walk the dark paths.

Ironically, the first emotion I felt when I was diagnosed with cancer was guilt. I felt that I had let so many people down—my husband and daughter, my employer, even God. Isn't it sad that guilt is so powerful in our lives? Feeling guilty keeps our focus off the real problem and potentially delays our healing. I had to press through those guilty feelings and believe God for my healing anyway.

I remember thinking, *If God loves me, why did this happen to me? What did I do to deserve this?* Some Christians would have you believe that if you are sick there is sin in your life. I searched and searched my heart, and even though I'm far from perfect—and certainly God is working on many areas of my life—I did not feel that I was living a lifestyle of sinful behavior. So where could I place the blame? If God didn't make me sick and my sin was not to blame, whom could I pin this on? The answer is we live in a fallen world and there are struggles every day. And bad things really do happen to good people. Thank God, Jesus bore the stripes for our healing and paid the price for our deliverance.

So I chose to use this time in my life as an opportunity to know God on a deeper level. Cancer caused me to question everything I had believed to be true. I believed I would live to be an old woman. I believed I would never be seriously ill. I believed God loved me. I believed God was a healer. After my cancer diagnosis, I had to truly decide if I still believed those things. Could I continue to believe God was a healer even though I was sick? Could I continue to believe God loved me when I felt so abandoned?

The answer is *yes*! I can continue to believe simply because God's Word is true. God is our healer, and he does love us. "For he has rescued us from the dominion of darkness and brought us into the kingdom of the Son he loves, in whom we have redemption, the forgiveness of sins" (Colossians 1:13–14).

I hope this journal has been a comfort to you. I pray for your health and your future, and although God is not the author of your illness, I believe he has healed you and placed you on earth "for such a time as this" (Esther 4:14). You are a living testimony of his goodness and mercy.

Remember to share your testimony of healing with others—it will encourage them and motivate them toward faith in God. You are a daughter of the Most High God. Never be ashamed of God's work in your life. "Always be prepared to give an answer to everyone who asks you to give the reason for the hope that you have" (1 Peter 3:15b). Be well, and rejoice in the Lord, always. And again I say, "*rejoice!*"

—Jane

"Though the mountains be shaken and the hills removed, yet my unfailing love for you will not be shaken nor my covenant of peace be removed," says the Lord, who has compassion on you.

Isaiah 54:10

Chemo Makes You Well

Cancer makes you sick.
Actually, chemo makes you sick,
But chemo makes you get well
And your hair will fall out.

Actually, chemo makes you sick,
But you'll live many more years
And your hair will fall out.
You'll get to see what you look like bald.

But you'll live many more years
And you'll get to see your grandchildren born.
You'll get to see what you look like bald.
And your hair might come back curly.

Cancer makes you sick,
But chemo makes you get well.
And you'll get to see your grandchildren born,
And your hair might come back curly.

—Jane Wilson

2004

Author Bio

At the age of forty, Jane Wilson found herself in an oncologist's office with a diagnosis of advanced breast cancer. After her cancer treatment was completed, she returned to college and completed a research project on the benefits of journaling, prayer, and meditation during cancer treatment. Jane is an accounting software consultant and trainer who has a degree in management and ethics and is currently pursuing an MBA at the University of Central Oklahoma. She lives in Edmond, Oklahoma, with her husband, Bill.

Made in the USA
Middletown, DE
25 September 2016